Bilingual Edition

LET'S LOOK AT FEELINGS™

Edición Bilingüe

What I Look Like When I Am

Sad

Cómo me veo cuando estoy

triste

Joanne Randolph
Traducción al español:
María Cristina Brusca

The Rosen Publishing Group's
PowerStart Press™ & **Editorial Buenas Letras**™
New York

1

Published in 2004 by The Rosen Publishing Group, Inc.
29 East 21st Street, New York, NY 10010

First Edition

Book Design: Kim Sonsky

Photo Credits: All photographs by Maura B. McConnell.

Library of Congress Cataloging-in-Publication Data

Randolph, Joanne.
[What I look like when I am sad. Spanish & English]
What I look like when I am sad = Como me veo cuando estoy triste / Joanne Randolph ; translated by Maria Cristina Brusca.— 1st ed.
    p. cm. — (Let's look at feelings)
Summary: Describes how the parts of the face look when a person is sad.
English and Spanish.
Includes bibliographical references and index.
ISBN 1-4042-7507-X (library binding)
1. Sadness in children—Juvenile literature. [1. Sadness. 2. Facial expression. 3. Emotions. 4. Spanish language material—Bilingual.] I. Title: Como me veo cuando estoy triste. II. Title. III. Series.

BF723.S15R3618 2004
152.4—dc21
                                        2003009108

Manufactured in the United States of America

Due to the changing nature of Internet links, PowerStart Press has developed an online list of Web sites related to the subject of this book. This site is updated regularly. Please use this link to access the list:

http://www.buenasletraslinks.com/llafe/triste/

Contents

Contenido

I am sad.

_____

Estoy triste.

5

When I am sad my head drops down.

Cuando estoy triste, bajo la cabeza.

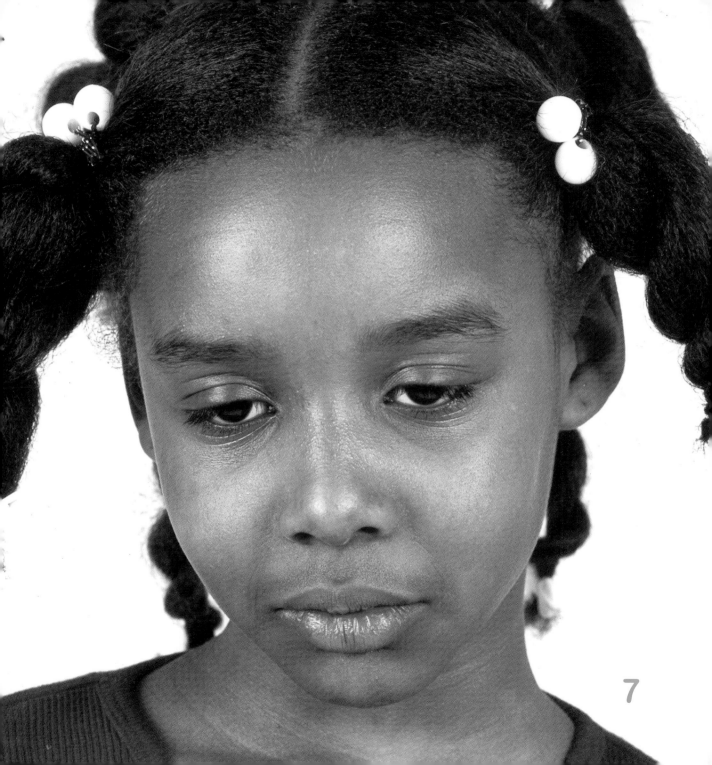

7

When I am sad my mouth
makes a frown.

Cuando estoy triste,
mi boca hace pucheros.

9

My bottom lip sticks out
when I am sad.

Cuando estoy triste,
mi labio inferior sale
para afuera.

11

When I am sad my eyebrows wrinkle.

Cuando estoy triste, mis cejas se arrugan.

13

My eyes look down
when I am sad.

Mis ojos miran hacia
abajo, cuando estoy triste.

15

When I am sad my
eyelids close.

Cuando estoy triste,
mis párpados se cierran.

When I am very sad I cry.

Cuando estoy muy triste, lloro.

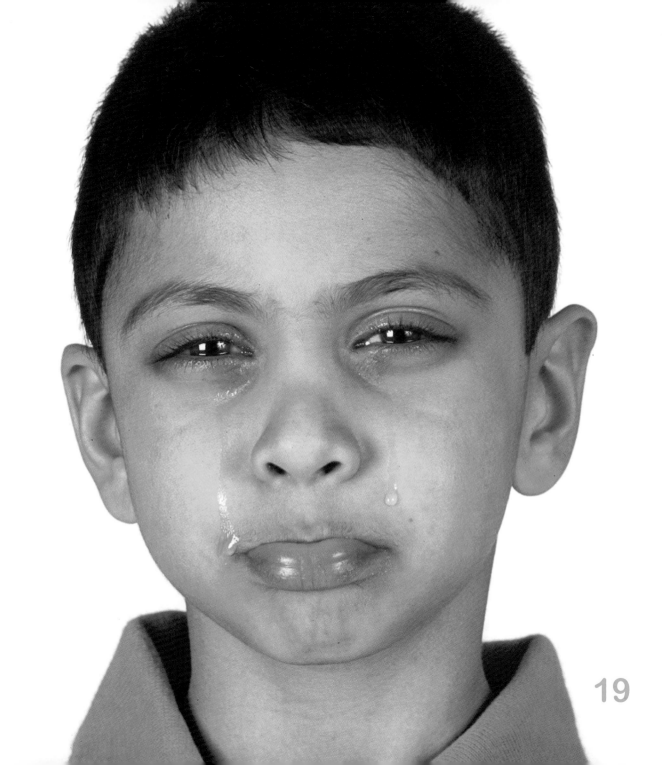

My eyes look red when I
am very sad.

Mis ojos se ponen rojos,
cuando estoy muy triste.

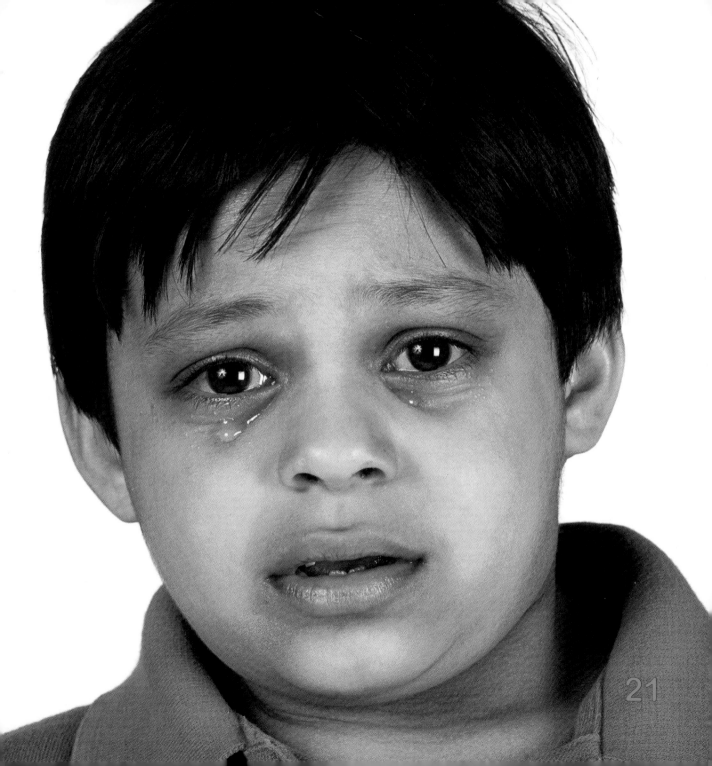

21

This is what I look like
when I am sad.

Así me veo cuando
estoy triste.

Words to Know
Palabras que debes saber

eyebrow
ceja

eyelid
párpado

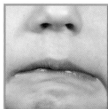

frown
puchero

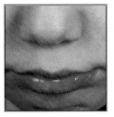

lip
labio

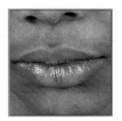

mouth
boca

wrinkle
arruga

Index

Índice

24